Cultural Traditions in
Canada

Molly
Aloian

Crabtree Publishing Company
www.crabtreebooks.com

Crabtree Publishing Company

www.crabtreebooks.com

Author: Molly Aloian
Publishing plan research and development:
  Reagan Miller
Editor: Kelly Spence
Proofreader and indexer: Wendy Scavuzzo
Design: Tibor Choleva
Photo research: Melissa McClellan
Proofreader: Marcia Abramson, Wendy Scavuzzo
Production coordinator and prepress technician:
  Tammy McGarr
Print coordinator: Margaret Amy Salter

Produced and Designed by BlueAppleWorks Inc.

Cover: Inukshuk at the Roundhouse at Whistler, Canada (background); The Canadian Royal Mounted Police (right center); Poutine (bottom right); Totem pole (bottom center); Eskimo woman wearing traditional clothing (left center); Loon (bottom right); Moose (top right)

Title page: Children in snow, with Rocky Mountains in the background

Photographs:
Dreamstime: © Barbara Helgason: title page (background); © Marzanna: title page (bottom); © Darren Baker: page 10, © Photka: page 30 (inset)
Keystone Press: ZUMAPRESS.com: page 7 (bottom), page 11 (bottom)
Toronto Star via Getty Images: page 14
Thinkstock: Ryan McVay: page 26
Library and Archives Canada: Bruce Moss/Weekend Magazine collection/e002852712: page 31 (top)
Shutterstock: Cover (all); © meunierd (bottom center); © Birdiegal (top right); © michelaubryphoto (bottom right); © TMore Campbell (bottom left); © Zoran Karapancev (right center); © bikeriderlondon (left center); © Bernard Zajac (background); © Vlad G: page 4; © Alexandra Demyanova: page 4 (bottom); © wong sze yuen: page 5; © Canadapanda: pages 6, 8, 28; © Sergei Bachlakov: pages 6 (inset), 8 (bottom), 16 (inset), 17, 25 (inset); © Maridav: page 9 (top & inset); © oliveromg: page 11 (top); © Vibe Images: page 11 (inset); © Josef Hanus: page 12; © Blend Images: page 13; © Elena Elisseeva: page 15 (top); © Bill Perry: page 15 (inset); © Goodluz: page 16; © David P. Lewis: page 18 (inset); © Alexander Mak: page 19 (inset); © RHIMAGE: pages 18-19 (background); © steve estvanik: pages 20, 21 (inset); © Muriel Lasure: page 20 (inset); © Jeff Whyte: page 21 (top); © Monkey Business Images: page 22; © ValeStock: page 23 (top), 24-25 (bottom); © Tatiana Volgutova: page 24-25 (background); © Brent Hofacker: page 25 (top); © Sandra van der Steen: page 27 (bottom); © picturepartners: page 27 (inset); © meunierd: pages 28 (inset), 29; © Daniel Dupuis: page 29 (inset); © Pressmaster: page 30 (bottom); © Werner Heiber: page 31 (bottom)
Wikimedia Commons: Kenny Louie: pages 7 (top); Public domain: page 23 (inset)

Library and Archives Canada Cataloguing in Publication

Aloian, Molly, author
  Cultural traditions in Canada / Molly Aloian.

(Cultural traditions in my world)
Includes index.
Issued in print and electronic formats.
ISBN 978-0-7787-0297-9 (bound).--ISBN 978-0-7787-0312-9 (pbk.).--ISBN 978-1-4271-7484-0 (html).--ISBN 978-1-4271-7490-1 (pdf)

  1. Holidays--Canada--Juvenile literature. 2. Canada--Social life and customs--Juvenile literature. I. Title. II. Series: Cultural traditions in my world

GT4813.A2A56 2014   j394.26971   C2014-900905-4
                                               C2014-900906-2

Library of Congress Cataloging-in-Publication Data

Aloian, Molly.
  Cultural traditions in Canada / Molly Aloian.
      pages cm. -- (Cultural traditions in my world)
  Includes index.
  ISBN 978-0-7787-0297-9 (reinforced library binding : alk. paper) -- ISBN 978-0-7787-0312-9 (pbk. : alk. paper) -- ISBN 978-1-4271-7490-1 (electronic pdf : alk. paper) -- ISBN 978-1-4271-7484-0 (electronic html : alk. paper)
  1. Holidays--Canada--Juvenile literature. 2. Festivals--Canada--Juvenile literature. 3. Canada--Social life and customs--Juvenile literature. I. Title.

GT4813.A2A46 2014
394.26971--dc23
                                               2014005116

Crabtree Publishing Company
www.crabtreebooks.com   1-800-387-7650

Printed in Canada/052020/CPC20200520

Published in Canada
Crabtree Publishing
616 Welland Ave.
St. Catharines, ON
L2M 5V6

Published in the United States
Crabtree Publishing
PMB 59051
350 Fifth Avenue, 59th Floor
New York, New York 10118

Published in the United Kingdom
Crabtree Publishing
Maritime House
Basin Road North, Hove
BN41 1WR

Published in Australia
Crabtree Publishing
3 Charles Street
Coburg North
VIC 3058

Contents

Welcome to Canada

Canada is one of the most **multicultural** countries in the world. Over 34 million people live in Canada. The country has two official languages—English and French. Many people **immigrate** to Canada from other countries. When they come to Canada, they often bring unique traditions with them from their native cultures.

Canada's capital city is Ottawa. This is the **Parliament** Building.

Cultural traditions are holidays, festivals, special days, and customs that groups of people celebrate. Some are religious celebrations and others honor an important day in history or carry on a long-standing custom. In Canada, many holidays and celebrations take place throughout the year that celebrate the country's history and **diversity**.

Did You Know?
Many **Muslims** living in Canada celebrate Ramadan. During this month-long holiday, Muslims pray, **fast**, and give to charity.

Happy New Year!

On December 31, many Canadians celebrate New Year's Eve. Celebrations take place across Canada, and include parties, music, dancing, parades, and fireworks displays. Many people stay up late and count down the seconds to midnight. For many, the new year starting on January 1 symbolizes a fresh start or new beginning.

Many people celebrate New Year's Eve at Toronto's Nathan Phillips Square.

Did You Know?
Many Chinese Canadians celebrate Chinese New Year in January or February. Chinese New Year is also known as the Spring Festival. On the Chinese calendar, it is the first day of the new year.

New Year's Day is a national holiday in all Canadian **provinces** and **territories**. All businesses and schools are closed. In some parts of Canada, a popular New Year's Day tradition is the Polar Bear Dip. Brave adults plunge into the new year with a chilly swim in a lake, river, or ocean.

The Québec Winter Carnival

The Québec Winter Carnival is a festival that takes place every year in Québec City from the end of January to mid-February. This two-week celebration of winter in Canada is known as the biggest winter carnival in the world!

A snowman character with a red cap leads the parades that wind through the city during the Québec Winter Carnival. He is known as Bonhomme Carnaval. The word "bonhomme" means "good man" in English.

Did You Know?
Winter celebrations in Québec began over 200 years ago. Long ago, many **settlers** from France were living in present-day Québec. Most were Roman Catholics, who had rowdy celebrations just before Lent, which is a period of fasting in the Christian religion. The Québec Winter Carnival was born out of these celebrations.

The carnival features concerts, parades, snow rafting, ice slides, ice sculptures, and even an ice palace. There are also dogsled races, ice canoe races, and other outdoor sporting events including snowboarding and hockey.

9

Family Day

Each year, many Canadians celebrate Family Day on the second or third Monday in February. People have the day off work and school to celebrate the importance of families and family life. Family members take part in fun activities such as going to movies or museums, playing board games, or doing crafts together. Some families go away for a long weekend. Family Day is also a good time to research your family's history.

Did You Know?
Family Day was first held in 1990 in the province of Alberta.

On Family Day some families enjoy winter activities such as building snowmen and tobogganing.

Did You Know?
In the province of Manitoba, the third Monday of February is Louis Riel Day. On this day, people honor and remember Louis Riel, the famous *Métis* leader who is known as the Father of Manitoba.

RIEL

Good Friday and Easter

Good Friday is celebrated two days before Easter. Easter takes place in March or April. On Good Friday, Christians commemorate the **crucifixion** of Jesus Christ. People go to special church services on Good Friday to mourn for Jesus Christ. On Easter Sunday, people celebrate the **resurrection** of Jesus Christ after his crucifixion.

Easter is the most sacred of all Christian holidays.

Kids can fill up their baskets during Easter egg hunts.

People also celebrate Easter with family and friends by sharing a special dinner. Easter egg hunts and decorating Easter eggs are popular Easter activities for kids. Children look forward to hunting for the colorful Easter eggs left by the Easter bunny. Many eggs have prizes inside.

Victoria Day

Victoria Day has been a holiday in Canada since 1845. Victoria Day is celebrated in honor of Queen Victoria's birthday. Victoria Day takes place on the Monday before May 25. In 1953, the Canadian government also declared this day a celebration of Queen Elizabeth II's birthday, although her actual birthday is April 2. Queen Elizabeth is the current **monarch** of Canada.

Many cities have Victoria Day parades and fireworks.

Victoria Day marks the end of the long, cold winter and the beginning of warmer spring weather in Canada. Many families go camping and open up their cottages for the summer season ahead.

Did You Know?
One of the most well-known Victoria Day parades takes place in the city of Victoria, British Columbia, which was named after Queen Victoria. Victoria was the queen of England when Canada was under British rule. A large statue in Victoria, British Columbia, honors her.

National Aboriginal Day

The first people to live in Canada were native people thousands of years ago. Today, Canadians celebrate National Aboriginal Day each year on June 21 to recognize and honor indigenous, or native, peoples and cultures. Native people also honor their **ancestors** on this day in June.

Many people go for hikes or canoe rides on National Aboriginal Day.

Dancing is part of the heritage of the First Nations who, along with Inuit, and Métis, make up the aboriginal, or native, peoples of Canada.

There are hundreds of special events across the country, which include music, singing, dancing, crafts, and storytelling. These events give many people the chance to learn more about native people and cultures throughout Canada and their many contributions and achievements.

Did You Know?
Long ago, many native people held special ceremonies or celebrations in the month of June, when the summer solstice happens. The summer solstice is the longest day of the year and the first day of summer. It is still celebrated by many people today.

17

Canada Day

On July 1, Canadians all around the country celebrate Canada's birthday. On this day in 1867, Canada officially became a country. Canadians celebrate their country's birthday with parades, barbecues, concerts, and fireworks.

Fireworks light up the sky over Ottawa to celebrate Canada Day.

Did You Know?
Some of the biggest Canada Day celebrations take place in Ottawa, which is Canada's capital city. Huge crowds of people gather near Parliament Hill and wave Canadian flags. There is a maple leaf in the middle of the Canadian flag because maple trees grow all over Canada.

Did You Know?
June 24 is Québec's National Day, or Fête nationale du Québec. People all over the province have parades, parties, bonfires, and set off fireworks to celebrate Québec's French culture.

This girl has a Canadian flag painted on her face for Canada Day.

The Calgary Stampede

The Calgary Stampede has been called "The Greatest Outdoor Show on Earth."

Every year, millions of people gather in Calgary, Alberta, for ten days in July. They gather at the Calgary Stampede, which is one of the biggest rodeos in the world. A rodeo is an exhibition of cowboy skills, such as roping cattle and riding horses. The Stampede celebrates the cowboys, farmers, and ranchers who helped shape life in western Canada.

Blackfoot Elders are opening the traditional Indian Village at the Calgary Stampede.

Did You Know?
In 1912, a famous cowboy and entertainer named Guy Weadick organized a festival and rodeo in Calgary. Over time, this event grew bigger and more popular. Today, it is better known as the Calgary Stampede.

Labor Day

Canadians celebrate Labor Day on the first Monday of September. On this national holiday, many families enjoy a last long weekend before the new school year begins. People may go on a camping trip, go to a cottage, or simply have an outdoor picnic or barbecue.

Did You Know?
The celebration of Labor Day began in Canada in 1872. Today, this holiday is celebrated in the United States, Australia, New Zealand, and other countries.

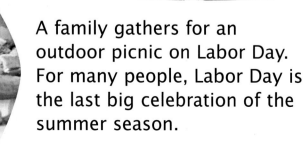

A family gathers for an outdoor picnic on Labor Day. For many people, Labor Day is the last big celebration of the summer season.

Workers and their families march in a modern Labor Day parade. The first Labor Day march (below) was held in Toronto in 1871!

Long ago, Labor Day was designated as the day for workers to ask for better working conditions or pay increases. Workers fought for their rights on Labor Day. They fought for eight hours of work, eight hours for recreation, and eight hours for rest. Today, this holiday commemorates the beginning of the eight-hour workday and the celebrates the many people who contribute to Canada's **economy**.

23

Happy Thanksgiving!

Thanksgiving Day has been an official holiday in Canada since 1957. On the second Monday of October, Canadians give thanks for the harvest of fall foods. They often spend the three-day weekend visiting family or friends, drinking apple cider and eating a traditional Thanksgiving meal of roast turkey, squash, turnips, and pumpkin pie. Thanksgiving weekend is also a perfect time to go for hikes or nature walks to admire the spectacular colors of the trees during the Canadian fall.

Different families have their own favorite Thanksgiving foods. What are your family's favorites?

Did You Know?
Native people in Canada held ceremonies and festivals to celebrate the fall harvest long before European explorers and settlers arrived in present-day Canada. They celebrated and gave thanks for all the gifts from the land.

Halloween

Each year, Canadians celebrate Halloween on October 31. This spooky holiday was brought to Canada by immigrants from Scotland and Ireland. Today, kids across Canada dress up as ghosts, witches, skeletons, or their other favorite characters, and go out trick-or-treating. They knock on the doors of their neighbors and say, "Trick-or-treat!" They are given candy and treats.

Kids go trick-or-treating. An adult should always stay nearby.

Today, many people across Canada carve pumpkins into jack-o'-lanterns to decorate their home. Pretend spiderwebs and bats also make good decorations. Some families get even more creative. They build make-believe dungeons or graveyards in their front yard! Costume parties for adults and children are part of the fun, too. Sometimes a whole neighborhood hosts a costume party.

Green face paint is the perfect finishing touch for witches.

Remembrance Day

Remembrance Day is a special day in Canada. On November 11 each year, people remember and honor the men and women who have served Canada during times of war. At 11 o'clock in the morning, two minutes of silence are observed across the country to remember the people who have fought and died. Their bravery and courage made a difference in Canada's future. They gave their lives so other Canadians could live in peace.

Flowers and Canadian flags are placed at a special monument called a cenotaph, or empty tomb, which honors fallen soldiers. No soldiers are actually buried there.

Many people wear red poppies in the weeks leading up to Remembrance Day. Poppies are symbols of Remembrance Day because they bloomed over the graves of dead soldiers.

Christmas in Canada

Canadians celebrate Christmas on December 25. For Christians, Christmas is a time to celebrate the birth of Jesus Christ. On Christmas Eve, many people go to church for special Christmas services. In the days leading up to Christmas, people decorate their homes with twinkly lights and Christmas trees. Family members exchange gifts and visit with friends and relatives on Christmas Eve or Christmas Day.

Families hang colorful ornaments and candy canes on Christmas trees.

During Christmastime in Newfoundland and Labrador, mummering is a popular tradition in many communities. Mummers are people who dress up in funny clothes and cover their faces. The mummers visit their families and friends and entertain them with dancing, music, and jokes. People try to guess the identity of the mummer underneath the costume.

Did You Know?
Boxing Day is celebrated in Canada on December 26. This is a popular day for Canadians to go shopping.

Glossary

ancestors People from whom others are descended

crucifixion Dying on a cross

diversity Having people of many different races or cultures

economy The system of producing, buying, and selling goods and services

fast To not eat food; often for religious reasons

immigrate To move from one country to another

Métis Aboriginal people in Canada with mixed native and European heritage

monarch A person who rules over a country or kingdom

multicultural Made up of several cultural or ethnic groups

Muslims People who believe in the religion of Islam

parliament The highest legislative body in some governments

provinces Areas of a country that have their own governments; in Canada, there are ten provinces

resurrection Coming back to life after death

settlers People who make their home in a new region

territories Areas that are run by a country's government; In Canada, there are three territories

Index